## TAKE-OFF!

*Transport Around the World*

# EMERGENCY VEHICLES

Chris Oxlade

Heinemann
**LIBRARY**

**www.heinemann.co.uk**
Visit our website to find out more information about Heinemann Library books.

To order:

 Phone 44 (0) 1865 888066

 Send a fax to 44 (0) 1865 314091

 Visit the Heinemann Bookshop at www.heinemann.co.uk to browse our catalogue and order online.

First published in Great Britain by Heinemann Library, Halley Court, Jordan Hill, Oxford OX2 8EJ
a division of Reed Educational and Professional Publishing Ltd.
Heinemann is a registered trademark of Reed Educational and Professional Publishing Ltd.

OXFORD  MELBOURNE  AUCKLAND
JOHANNESBURG  BLANTYRE  GABORONE
IBADAN  PORTSMOUTH (NH) USA  CHICAGO

Designed by Paul Davies and Associates
Originated by Ambassador Litho Ltd
Printed and bound by South China Printing in Hong Kong/China

ISBN 0 431 13413 8 (hardback)          ISBN 0 431 13418 9 (paperback)
06 05 04 03 02                         06 05 04 03 02
10 9 8 7 6 5 4 3 2 1                   10 9 8 7 6 5 4 3 2 1

**British Library Cataloguing in Publication Data**

Oxlade, Chris
    Emergency vehicles. – (Transport around the world) (Take-off!)
    1.Emergency vehicles – Juvenile literature
    I.Title
    629.2'25

**Acknowledgements**
The publishers would like to thank the following for permission to reproduce photographs:
R D Battersby pp12; Trevor Clifford pp22, 28; Corbis pp20, 21, 23; Mary Evans Picture Library p9; Eye Ubiquitous pp10, 19; PA Photos p27; Photodisc pp14, 15; Quadrant pp16, 17, 26, 29; Royal Navy p18; Science Museum p8; Shout Picture Library pp4, 5, 6, 7, 11; Tony Stone Images p13; TRH: Canadair pp 24, 25.

Cover photograph reproduced with permission of Alvey and Towers.

Our thanks to Sue Graves and Hilda Reed for their advice and expertise in the preparation of this book.

Every effort has been made to contact copyright holders of any material reproduced in this book. Any omissions will be rectified in subsequent printings if notice is given to the publishers.

# Contents

Any words appearing in the text in bold,
**like this**, are explained in the Glossary.

# What is an emergency vehicle?

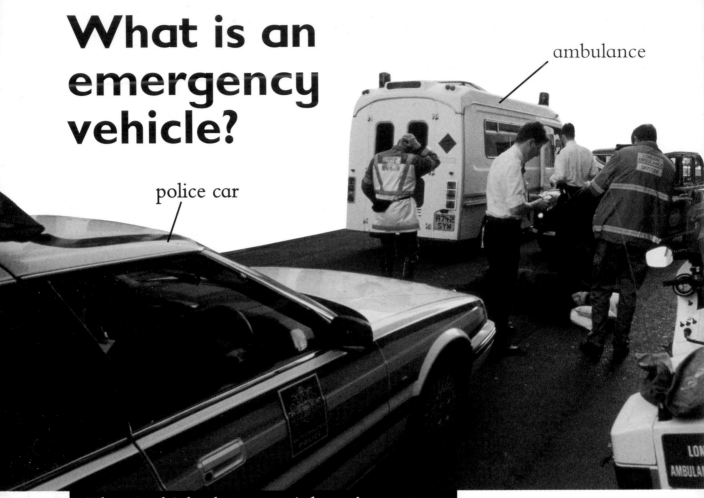

ambulance

police car

These vehicles have special **equipment** that helps with the rescue.

An emergency vehicle rushes to an accident to help **rescue** people. Cars, trucks, planes and boats can all be emergency vehicles.

Emergency vehicles have a **crew** who drive the vehicle and work its equipment.

The cutting equipment works like a huge pair of scissors to cut through twisted metal.

This fire engine crew is cutting open a car to rescue the driver.

cutting equipment

crew members

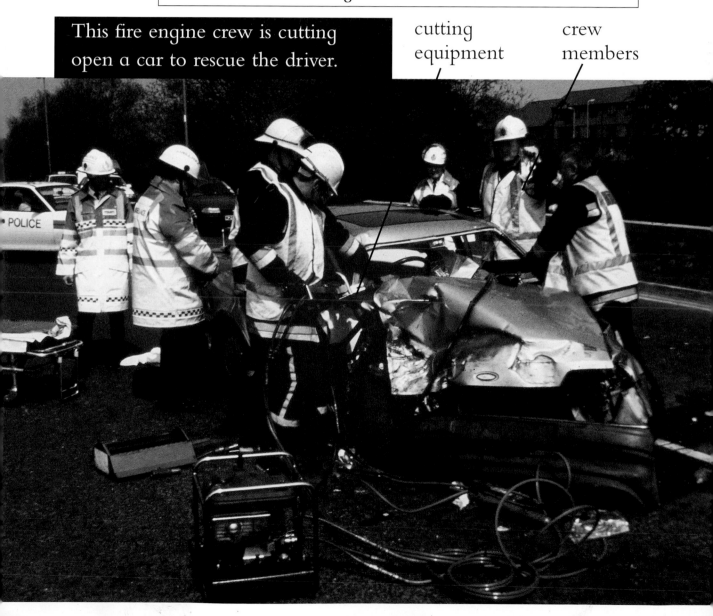

# Special parts

two-way radio

policeman

This policeman is using his two-way radio.

The police force first used two-way radio cars in 1927.

In the **cab** of an emergency vehicle there is a **two-way radio**. Using the radio, the crew can talk to a control centre. People at the control centre tell the **crew** where the emergencies are.

Emergency vehicles have flashing lights and loud **sirens** so that people know when they are coming.

Police, fire and ambulance vehicles in Britain have blue flashing lights.

Emergency vehicles often have floodlights like this for night-time emergencies.

floodlight

# Emergency vehicles long ago

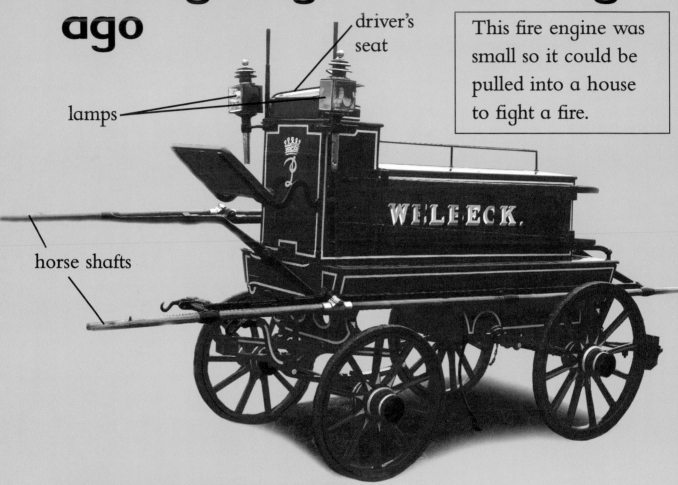

driver's seat

lamps

This fire engine was small so it could be pulled into a house to fight a fire.

horse shafts

WELBECK.

Fire engines like this one were pulled by horses.

This fire engine was built in 1866 and was pulled along by horses. Its crew pumped water to the fire by moving handles up and down.

Old lifeboats did not have **engines**. The crew had to row hard to get out to sea.

Ordinary fishing boats were used to rescue people at sea until the 1780s. The first specially designed lifeboat was built in 1770.

This old picture shows how hard it was to get into a lifeboat.

crew

lifeboat

# Where are emergency vehicles used?

This American police car is racing through the streets of New York City.

Police **patrol** cars, ambulances and fire engines travel on roads. They often have to rush through busy traffic. The driver needs to be skilled and careful.

helicopter

Helicopters can reach places where there are no roads. Rescue boats travel on water to reach people who need help.

Helicopters do not have to land for a rescue.

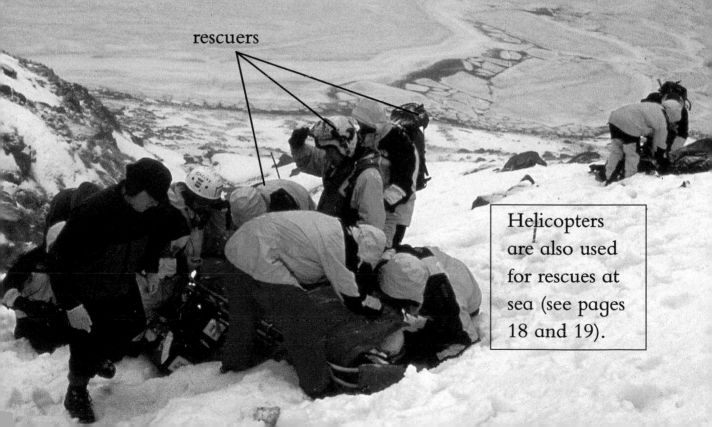

rescuers

Helicopters are also used for rescues at sea (see pages 18 and 19).

# Police patrol cars

Police officers **patrol** the streets of towns and cities in patrol cars. Some patrol cars have powerful **engines** so that the officers can reach the accident quickly.

This patrol car has a powerful engine.

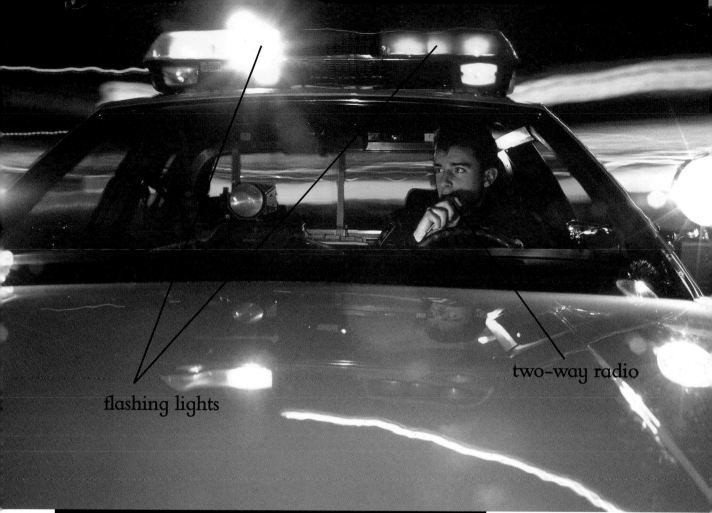

two-way radio

flashing lights

This police officer is using his **two-way radio**.

In an emergency, a police officer will switch on the patrol car's flashing lights and sirens so that other drivers can get out of the way.

Police officers started to use two-way radios on the beat in 1965. How long ago was that?

# Ambulances

An ambulance is a vehicle that carries ill or injured people to hospital. Inside the ambulance there is space to put a person on a **stretcher**.

flashing lights

ambulance

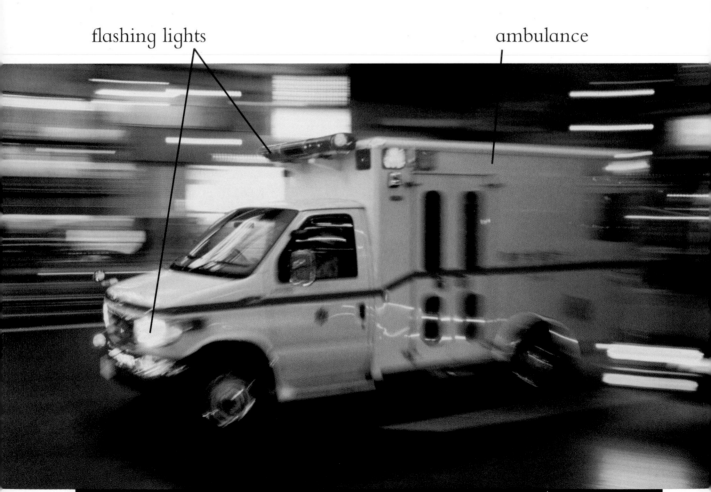

This ambulance is rushing to get an injured person to hospital.

crew
member

injured
person

first aid
equipment

The crew use first aid **equipment** to help the injured person.

Ambulances today are like small hospitals inside.

The ambulance driver and **crew** are trained to use **first aid**. They treat the injured person as the ambulance travels to hospital.

# Flying doctors

In Australia, may people live in remote areas called the outback. Ambulances cannot reach them quickly. The Flying Doctor Service uses special planes that fly people to hospital.

This plane is part of the Flying Doctor Service.

plane

On board the planes are beds and equipment.

On board the planes are beds for patients. There is also **equipment** that doctors can use to treat patients.

The first flying doctor was a man called Dr K. St Vincent Welch. You can find out more about the Flying Doctor Service on page 30.

# Helicopters

spinning
rotor

sea cliffs

The helicopter is lifted into the air by its spinning **rotor**.

This is an air-sea **rescue** helicopter. It rescues people who are in trouble at sea or in the mountains.

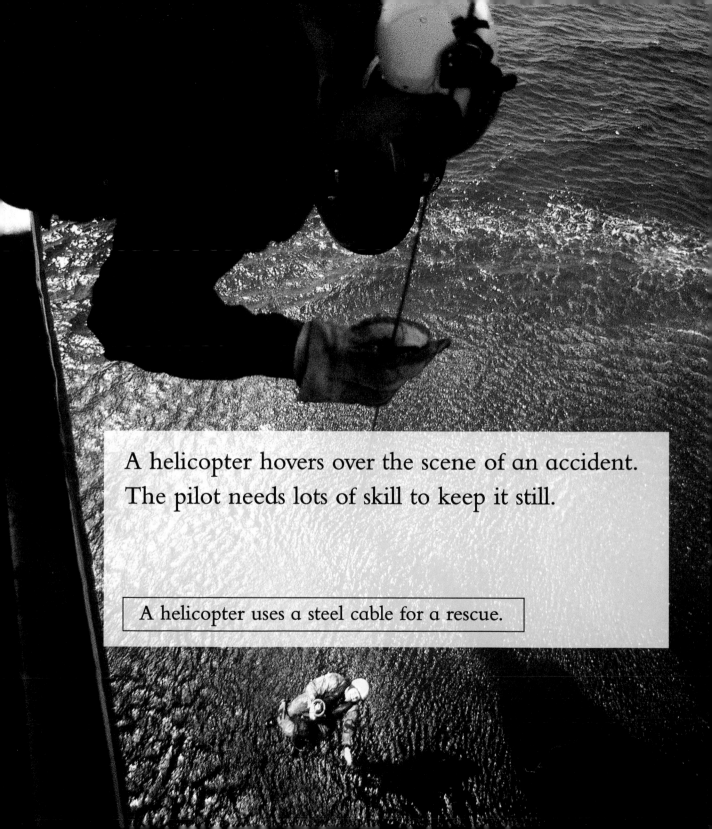

A helicopter hovers over the scene of an accident.
The pilot needs lots of skill to keep it still.

A helicopter uses a steel cable for a rescue.

# Lifeboats

If a modern lifeboat **capsizes**, it will right itself.

Lifeboats can go safely through enormous waves.

waves

A lifeboat is a boat that **rescues** people from sinking boats and ships. Lifeboats are fast and strong.

A lifeboat must get to sea as quickly as possible when its **crew** get an emergency call.

The Royal National Lifeboat Institution was founded in 1824. It organizes sea rescues.

This lifeboat slides down a steep ramp straight into the waves.

crew

ramp

SELSEY LIFE BOAT

lifeboat

# Fire engines

flashing lights     crew member     ladders     hose

This is an American fire engine.

A fire engine carries lots of fire-fighting **equipment**, such as long ladders and water hoses.

> The water tank on a fire engine can carry 1800 litres of water!

Some fire engines have a huge **tank** of water and a powerful water **pump**. Strong hoses can carry water from the pump or water pipe to the fire.

A fire engine carries lots of equipment.

ladders

hoses

crew member

N437 CBW

EXCALIBUR

# Water bombers

Some special fire-fighting planes drop water on to a forest fire. Normal fire engines cannot get to the fire through the thick forest.

The water tank on a fire-fighting plane can carry 1000 litres of water.

This plane is water-bombing a forest fire.

plane

water

forest

fire

plane    water tank

The pilot skims over the lake to scoop up water.

This fire-fighting plane has a big water tank inside. The pilot fills it by skimming over a lake and scooping up water.

# Airport fire engines

spray gun

crew member

fire engine

ท่าอากาศยานกรุงเทพ
BANGKOK INTERNATIONAL AIRPORT

4

Fire engines are on stand-by at airports around the world.

This fire engine is used at Bangkok airport in Thailand. Find Thailand on a map of the world.

Every airport has its own fire engines like this one. They are always ready to rush to the **rescue** in case a plane has an accident.

An airport fire engine has a spray gun on the roof. The gun sprays thick foam over a crashed plane. This keeps out **oxygen** and stops the fire spreading.

Thick foam stops fire on a plane from spreading.

fire engine

spray gun

crashed plane

foam

# Breakdown trucks

A breakdown truck goes to **rescue** cars, trucks and buses that have broken down.

New York is called the 'The Big Apple', so it is easy to see why this breakdown service is called 'Apple Towing'!

breakdown truck

This is an American breakdown truck.

mechanic

car ramp

breakdown truck

The car is winched up the ramp.

A **mechanic** uses the tools on a breakdown truck to mend the broken vehicle. If it cannot be mended, it is put on the back of the truck to be taken to a garage. A **winch** pulls the car up a ramp at the back of a truck.

# Timeline

| | | |
|---|---|---|
| 1800 | 1800s | Fire engines are pulled by horses or firemen. Their pumps are worked by firemen using their hands or feet. |
| | 1824 | The world's first lifeboat service is started in the UK. It uses self-righting lifeboats that were rowed to sea by the crew. |
| 1850 | 1850s | The first ambulances are used during the Crimean War. They are horse-drawn carts with stretchers on top. |
| | 1885 | The first proper car is built in Germany by Karl Benz. It has three wheels and is driven along by a petrol engine. Top speed is 13 kilometres per hour. |
| 1900 | | |
| | 1928 | In Australia, the Royal Flying Doctor Service is started. It carries doctors to remote towns in the Australian outback. |
| | 1940 | The first successful helicopter makes a flight. It is the Sikorsky VS-300, designed by Igor Sikorsky. |
| 1950 | | |
| | 1967 | The Canadair CL-215 water bomber makes its first flight in Canada. It is designed to drop water on forest fires. |
| 2000 | | |

# Glossary

a
b
c
d
e
f
g
h
i
j
k
l
m
n
o
p
q
r
s
t
u
v
w
x
y
z

**cab**  space at the front of a van or truck where the driver sits

**capsize**  overturn

**crew**  group of people working together

**engine**  machine that uses fuel to make a vehicle move

**equipment**  machines and supplies that help people do a job

**first aid**  helping someone who is injured, before they get to hospital

**mechanic**  person who mends vehicles and their engines

**oxygen**  a gas in the air that helps things burn

**patrol**  travel around a town or city looking for emergencies

**pump**  a machine that moves water

**rescue**  save from danger

**rotor**  blade that spins round on a helicopter

**siren**  device that makes a loud warning noise

**stretcher**  simple bed for ill or injured people that can be carried by two people

**tank**  large container for storing something, such as water

**two-way radio**  radio that lets you talk and listen to someone else

**winch**  machine that pulls in a cable, like the reel on a fishing rod

31

# Index

a b c d e f g h i j k l m n o p q r s t u v w x y z